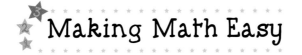

Making Math Easy

Multiplication Made Easy

Rebecca Wingard-Nelson

DO NOT FEED THE PIRANHA

$$\begin{array}{r} 6 \\ \times 3 \\ \hline 18 \end{array}$$

Enslow Elementary

an imprint of

Enslow Publishers, Inc.

40 Industrial Road   PO Box 38
Box 398   Aldershot
Berkeley Heights, NJ 07922   Hants GU12 6BP
USA   UK

http://www.enslow.com

Enslow Elementary, an imprint of Enslow Publishers, Inc.

Enslow Elementary® is a registered trademark of Enslow Publishers, Inc.

Library of Congress Cataloging-in-Publication Data

Wingard-Nelson, Rebecca.
  Multiplication made easy / Rebecca Wingard-Nelson.
      p. cm. — (Making math easy)
  Includes index.
  ISBN 0-7660-2510-1 (hardcover)
  1. Multiplication—Juvenile literature. I. Title.
  QA115.W77 2005
  513.2'13—dc22

                                        2004021659

Printed in the United States of America

10 9 8 7 6 5 4 3 2

To Our Readers: We have done our best to make sure all Internet Addresses in this book were active and appropriate when we went to press. However, the author and the publisher have no control over and assume no liability for the material available on those Internet sites or on other Web sites they may link to. Any comments or suggestions can be sent by e-mail to comments@enslow.com or to the address on the back cover.

Illustrations: Tom LaBaff

Cover illustration: Tom LaBaff

Contents

Introduction

Math is all around, and an important part of anyone's life. You use math when you are playing games, cooking food, spending money, telling time, reading music, or doing any other activity that uses numbers. Even finding a television channel uses math!

Multiplication Is Everywhere

You need multiplication in everyday life. It is used when you count things that are in groups or rows, when you need to know the area of a room or space, and when you need to know how much money it will cost to buy more than one of something.

Using This Book

This book can be used to learn or review multiplication at your own speed. It can be used on your own or with a friend, tutor, or parent. Get ready to discover math . . . made easy!

Multiplication is just another way to repeatedly add a number.

You have five containers of tennis balls, and each container has four balls. How many tennis balls do you have?

There are two ways to find the answer. You can find the total by adding the number of tennis balls in each container.

$$4 + 4 + 4 + 4 + 4 = 20$$

Or you can multiply.

4 added 5 times is 20.

This can be written as

4 times 5 is 20, or $4 \times 5 = 20$.

Multiplication?

Kaylee planted three rows of corn with six plants in each row. How many plants did Kaylee have in all?

$$6 + 6 + 6 = 18$$

6 added 3 times is 18.

6 times 3 is 18.

$$6 \times 3 = 18.$$

Multiplication is repeated addition.

Multiplication

You can write multiplication problems in two ways, in a line or in a column.

line
$$2 \times 3 = 6$$

column
$$\begin{array}{r} 2 \\ \times\, 3 \\ \hline 6 \end{array}$$

The $\times$ means "multiply." The $\times$ is sometimes read as "times." The $=$ means "equals." The line in column multiplication also means "equals."

When you read a multiplication problem out loud, you say

$$2 \quad \times \quad 3 \quad = \quad 6$$

"Two times three equals six," or

"Two multiplied by three equals six."

Terms

The numbers being multiplied are called factors.

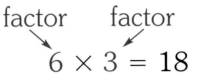

$$6 \times 3 = 18$$

The answer to a multiplication problem is called the product.

product

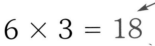

$$6 \times 3 = 18$$

Multiplication

Multiplication tables show mutiplication facts. This table shows the multiplication facts for the numbers 0 through 12. You can use a multiplication table when you do not remember a basic multiplication fact.

	0	1	2	3	4	5	6	7	8	9	10	11	12
0	0	0	0	0	0	0	0	0	0	0	0	0	0
1	0	1	2	3	4	5	6	7	8	9	10	11	12
2	0	2	4	6	8	10	12	14	16	18	20	22	24
3	0	3	6	9	12	15	18	21	24	27	30	33	36
4	0	4	8	12	16	20	24	28	32	36	40	44	48
5	0	5	10	15	20	25	30	35	40	45	50	55	60
6	0	6	12	18	24	30	36	42	48	54	60	66	72
7	0	7	14	21	28	35	42	49	56	63	70	77	84
8	0	8	16	24	32	40	48	56	64	72	80	88	96
9	0	9	18	27	36	45	54	63	72	81	90	99	108
10	0	10	20	30	40	50	60	70	80	90	100	110	120
11	0	11	22	33	44	55	66	77	88	99	110	121	132
12	0	12	24	36	48	60	72	84	96	108	120	132	144

Tables

Let's look at **3 × 4**.

Find the first number, **3**, in the top row.

Find the second number, **4**, in the left column.

Move down from the **3** and across from the **4** to the box where the row and column meet. This box has the answer.

$$3 \times 4 = 12$$

	0	1	2	③	4
0	0	0	0	0	0
1	0	1	2	3	4
2	0	2	4	6	8
3	0	3	6	9	12
④	0	4	8	**12**	16
5	0	5	10	15	20

I like this table stuff.

Multiplication

Multiplication with zero is easy! Zero times any number is always zero.

If you have three plates with zero green beans on each plate, you have zero green beans.

$$0 + 0 + 0 = 0$$
$$3 \times 0 = 0$$

If you have zero plates with 400 green beans on each plate, you have zero green beans.

$$0 \times 400 = 0$$

and Zero

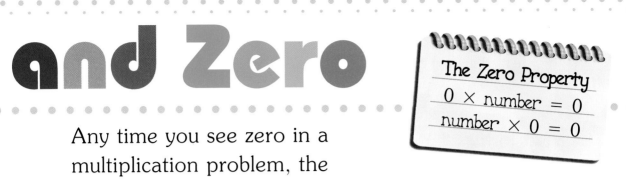

The Zero Property
$0 \times \text{number} = 0$
$\text{number} \times 0 = 0$

Any time you see zero in a multiplication problem, the answer is zero. This is called the zero property.

The zero property is true with every number.

$$1 \times 0 = 0 \qquad 0 \times 5 = 0$$
$$1{,}789 \times 0 = 0 \qquad 0 \times 327 = 0$$

Gwen is writing a story. She has six pages with zero words on each page. How many words has she written so far?

Multiply the number of pages by the number of words on each page.

$$6 \text{ pages} \times 0 \text{ words on each page}$$
$$6 \times 0 = 0$$

Gwen has written zero words so far.

Multiplication

Any time you see the number 1 in a multiplication problem, the answer is the same as the other number. This is called the property of one.

One row of six stars is six stars.

$$1 \times 6 = 6$$

Three groups of one fish are three fish.

$$3 \times 1 = 3$$

and One

The Property of One
1 × number = number
number × 1 = number

The property of one is true with every number.

$$1 \times 3 = 3$$
$$4{,}208 \times 1 = 4{,}208$$

Brent's job is to wash the chalkboards in the classrooms of the elementary school every day. There are 16 classrooms, and each has one chalkboard. How many chalkboards does Brent wash every day?

Multiply the number of classrooms by the number of chalkboards in each classroom.

16 classrooms × 1 chalkboard in each

$$16 \times 1 = 16$$

Brent washes 16 chalkboards every day.

Facts and

Basic multiplication facts are sometimes divided into groups using one of the factors. For example, all of the basic facts that use the number 2 are called the TWOs facts.

factor—A number that is multiplied with another number.

A hint to learn the TWOs facts is that two times any number is double the number.

$$2 \times 1 = 2$$ Double 1 is 2
$$2 \times 6 = 12$$ Double 6 is 12

When a number and any other number are multiplied, the answer is called a multiple. The multiples of two are the numbers you get when you mutliply any number and two.

Multiples

Use the TWOs facts to find five multiples of 2.

$$2 \times 1 = 2$$
$$2 \times 2 = 4$$
$$2 \times 3 = 6$$
$$2 \times 4 = 8$$
$$2 \times 5 = 10$$

multiples

HINT: All of the multiples of two are even numbers.

Five multiples of 2 are 2, 4, 6, 8, and 10.

Now find five multiples of 3.

$$3 \times 3 = 9$$
$$3 \times 4 = 12$$
$$3 \times 5 = 15$$
$$3 \times 6 = 18$$
$$3 \times 7 = 21$$

Five multiples of 3 are 9, 12, 15, 18, and 21.

Basic Fact

Here are some more hints to help you with multiplication.

FOUR times any number is double-double that number.

$4 \times 3 = 12$ Double 3 is 6, double 6 is 12

$4 \times 7 = 28$ Double 7 is 14, double 14 is 28

FIVEs facts can be memorized by counting by fives.

$5 \times 3 = 15$ Count by fives to the third number. 5, 10, 15

$5 \times 8 = 40$ Count by fives to the eighth number. 5, 10, 15, 20, 25, 30, 35, 40

HINT: When 5 and an even number are multiplied, the answer always ends in 0. When 5 and an odd number are multiplied, the answer always ends in 5.

Hints

The NINEs facts are fun! Hold up both of your hands with all ten fingers raised. Suppose you need to find the fact for 9×4. You are multiplying by 4, so put down the fourth finger from the left.

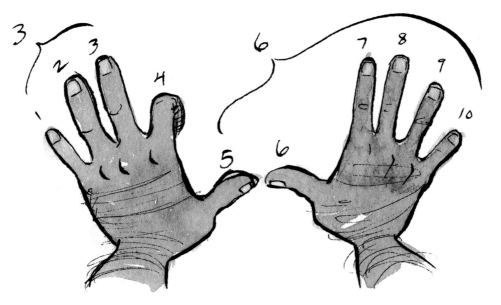

There are 3 fingers to the left of the fourth finger; these are the tens (30). To the right of the fourth finger, there are 6 fingers; these are the ones (6).

$$9 \times 4 = 36$$

This trick always works!

HINT: In the answer to a NINEs fact, the tens and ones digits always add up to nine. $9 \times 4 = 36$, so $3 + 6 = 9$.

Multiples

Multiplying numbers that end in zeros is simple once you know the basic facts.

$$6 \times 40 = \underline{}$$

Drop the zero. $\quad\quad\quad 6 \times 4\cancel{0}$

Find the basic fact. $\quad\quad 6 \times 4 = 24$

Put the zero back, and $\quad 6 \times 40 = 240$
add the zero to the answer.

This works no matter how many zeros are after the basic fact.

$$800 \times 2 = \underline{}$$

Drop the zeros. $\quad\quad\quad 8\cancel{0}\cancel{0} \times 2$

Find the basic fact. $\quad\quad 8 \times 2 = 16$

Put the zeros back, and $\quad 800 \times 2 = 1,600$
add the zeros to the answer.

You can drop the zeros even when there are zeros in both factors.

300 × 30

Drop the zeros. You are dropping three zeros.   3̶0̶0̶ × 3̶0̶

This is just TEMPORARY!

Find the basic fact.
3 × 3 = 9

Put the zeros back. Since you dropped three zeros, add three zeros to the answer.

300 × 30 = 9,000

Commutative

You can use the same numbers to make different multiplication problems. Let's try the numbers 5 and 6.

$$5 \times 6 = 30$$
$$6 \times 5 = 30$$

When the numbers being multiplied change places, the answer stays the same. This is called the commutative property of multiplication.

You can remember the name of the property by knowing that when you commute, you go back and forth, or change places.

You can have 6 groups of 5, or 5 groups of 6, and still have 30 all together.

Property

This property makes memorizing the multiplication facts easier. If you know the fact for 4×8, you also know the fact for 8×4.

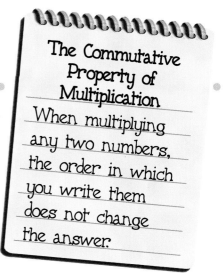

The Commutative Property of Multiplication

When multiplying any two numbers, the order in which you write them does not change the answer.

$$4 \times 8 = 32$$
$$8 \times 4 = 32$$

You can change the order of the numbers to check your answer to a multiplication problem.

$$9 \times 3$$

You think the answer is 27. Check your answer by changing the order of the numbers. What is 3×9? 27. Your first answer is correct.

$$9 \times 3 = 27$$

Associative

When you multiply more than two numbers, the order in which you multiply them does not change the answer.

$$3 \times 2 \times 4$$

Parentheses are used to group the numbers that get multiplied first.

The numbers 3 and 2 are multiplied first.

$$(3 \times 2) \times 4$$

Multiply inside the parentheses.

$$(3 \times 2) \times 4$$

Multiply the remaining numbers.

$$(6) \times 4 = 24$$

Now group a different set of numbers.

The numbers 2 and 4 are multiplied first.

$$3 \times (2 \times 4)$$

Multiply inside the parentheses.

$$3 \times (2 \times 4)$$

Multiply the remaining numbers.

$$3 \times (8) = 24$$

Property

$$(3 \times 2) \times 4 = 3 \times (2 \times 4)$$

The product did not change when the factors were grouped in different ways.

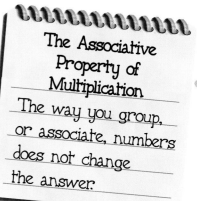

The Associative Property of Multiplication

The way you group, or associate, numbers does not change the answer.

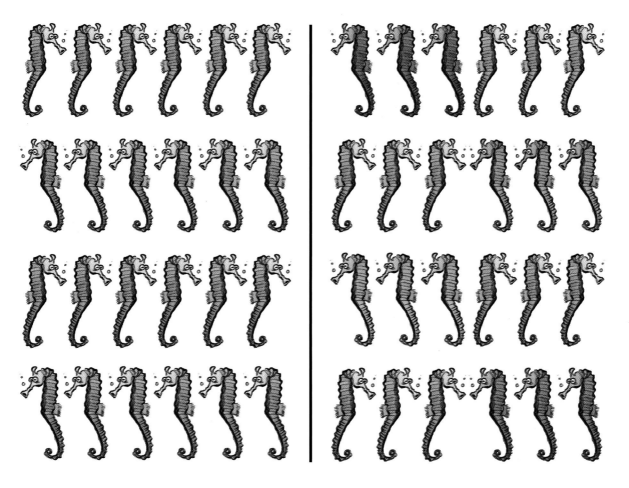

Distributive

When you are distributing papers, you are passing them out. The distributive property "passes out" multiplication to each of the numbers in an addition or subtraction problem.

$$6 \times (1 + 8)$$

You can solve this problem in two ways.

1 Do the addition inside the parentheses first, then multiply.

$$6 \times (1 + 8) = 6 \times (9) = 54$$

2 "Pass out" or distribute the multiplication, then add.

1. Multiply 6 by the first addend, 1.
2. Multiply 6 by the second addend, 8.
3. Add the two products.

$$
\begin{aligned}
6 \times (1 + 8) &= (6 \times 1) + (6 \times 8) \\
&= \quad (6) \quad + \quad (48) \\
&= \qquad\qquad 54
\end{aligned}
$$

No matter which way you solve it, the answer is 54.

Property

You can use this property to find multiplication facts you have not memorized yet.

$$8 \times (2 + 5) = 8 \times 7 = 56$$

If you do not know 8×7, you can distribute first.

$$
\begin{aligned}
8 \times (2 + 5) &= (8 \times 2) + (8 \times 5) \\
&= (16) + (40) \\
&= 56
\end{aligned}
$$

Multiplying

You can multiply any number by a one-digit number using place value.

$$412 \times 2$$

Separate the number 412 by place value.

You have 4 hundreds, 1 ten, and 2 ones.

Multiply each place by 2, beginning with ones.

2×2 ones = 4 ones, or 4
2×1 ten = 2 tens, or 20
2×4 hundreds = 8 hundreds, or 800

Now add the products.

$$\begin{array}{r} 4 \\ 20 \\ + \ 800 \\ \hline 824 \end{array}$$

$$412 \times 2 = 824$$

by One Digit

One-digit multiplication can be easy when you write the problem in columns.

32 × 3

place value—The value of a digit in a number. In the number 23, the digit 2 is in the tens place. Its place value is 2 tens.

Line up the numbers so that the same place values are in the same column.

$$\begin{array}{r} 32 \\ \times\ 3 \\ \hline \end{array}$$

Multiply the ones place.
2 × 3 = 6.
Write the answer in the ones column.

$$\begin{array}{r} 32 \\ \times\ 3 \\ \hline 6 \end{array}$$

Multiply the tens place.
3 × 3 = 9.
Write the answer in the tens column.

$$\begin{array}{r} 32 \\ \times\ 3 \\ \hline 96 \end{array}$$

32 × 3 = 96

Regrouping and

When the product in a place is more than nine, you can regroup to the next larger place.

56 × 4

Write the problem in columns.
Multiply ones. 6 × 4 = 24.
Regroup 24 as 2 tens and 4 ones.
Write 4 in the ones place.
Carry the 2 tens to the tens column.

$$\begin{array}{r} 2 \\ 56 \\ \times\ 4 \\ \hline 4 \end{array}$$

Multiply tens. 5 × 4 = 20.
Then add the regrouped 2 tens.
20 tens + 2 tens = 22 tens.

Cross out the regrouped 2 to show you have done the addition.

There are no more places to multiply, so write 22 tens, or 2 hundreds, 2 tens.

$$56 \times 4 = 224$$

Multiplication

Let's look at another one.

$$
\begin{array}{r}
\overset{4}{415} \\
\times\ 8 \\
\hline
0
\end{array}
\qquad
\begin{array}{r}
\overset{1\,4}{415} \\
\times\ 8 \\
\hline
20
\end{array}
\qquad
\begin{array}{r}
\overset{1\,4}{4}15 \\
\times\ 8 \\
\hline
3320
\end{array}
$$

Multiply ones.
$8 \times 5 = 40$.
Regroup.

Multiply tens.
$8 \times 1 = 8$.
Add.
$8 + 4 = 12$.
Regroup.

Multiply hundreds.
$8 \times 4 = 32$.
Add.
$32 + 1 = 33$.

3,320...

Multiplying

Two-digit multiplication problems can be solved by multiplying by one digit at a time.

91 × 47

Multiply 91 by the ones digit of the number 47, which is 7. The answer is called a partial product, because it is part of the total product.

Find another partial product by multiplying 91 by the tens digit of the number 47.

Multiply the tens. Since you are multiplying by 40, put a zero in the ones place. (See pages 20 and 21.) Multiply 91 by the tens digit, 4. Write the answer beginning in the tens column.

by Two Digits

Add the partial products.

$$637 + 3{,}640 = 4{,}277$$

$$91 \times 47 = 4{,}277$$

More Two-Digit

Columns can keep two-digit multiplication problems organized.

56 × 82

$$\begin{array}{r} \overset{\cancel{1}}{56} \\ \times\ 82 \\ \hline 112 \end{array}$$

Write the problem in columns according to place value. Multiply 56 by the ones digit, 2. $2 \times 6 = 12$. Regroup the 1. $2 \times 5 = 10$. $10 + 1 = 11$. The partial product is 112.

$$\begin{array}{r} \overset{\cancel{4}}{\overset{\cancel{1}}{56}} \\ \times\ 82 \\ \hline 112 \\ 4480 \end{array}$$

Now multiply the tens. Since you are really multiplying by 80, put a zero in the ones place directly below the first partial product. Now multiply. $8 \times 6 = 48$. Write the 8 in the tens column. Regroup the 4. $8 \times 5 = 40$. $40 + 4 = 44$. The second partial product is 4480.

Multiplication

The partial products are now neatly lined up by place value, ready to be added.

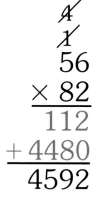

$$
\begin{array}{r}
56 \\
\times\ 82 \\
\hline
112 \\
+\ 4480 \\
\hline
4592
\end{array}
$$

All of the numbers below the first line are partial products.

Draw a second line below the partial products and add.

$$56 \times 82 = 4{,}592$$

Greater

Numbers that have more than two digits are also multiplied using partial products.

211 × 341

$$211$$
$$\times\ 341$$
$$\overline{211}$$

Write the problem in columns.
Multiply 211 by the ones digit, 1.
Write the partial product.

$$211$$
$$\times\ 341$$
$$\overline{211}$$
$$8440$$

Multiply 211 by the tens digit. Remember, since you are really multiplying by 40, put a zero in the ones place directly below the first partial product. Write the answer beginning in the tens column.

Numbers

$$
\begin{array}{r}
211 \\
\times\ 341 \\
\hline
211 \\
8440 \\
63300
\end{array}
$$

Multiply 211 by the hundreds digit. Since you are really multiplying by 300, put zeros in the ones and tens places below the second partial product. Write the answer beginning in the hundreds column.

$$
\begin{array}{r}
211 \\
\times\ 341 \\
\hline
211 \\
8440 \\
+\ 63300 \\
\hline
71951
\end{array}
$$

All of the numbers below the line are partial products. There are three digits in the second factor, so there are three partial products. Draw a line below the partial products and add them.

$$211 \times 341 = 71{,}951$$

Multiplying

Some numbers, such as 102 and 301, have zero as one of the digits. How do you multiply with these numbers?

$$301 \times 5$$

$$
\begin{array}{r}
301 \\
\times \quad 5 \\
\hline
5
\end{array}
$$

Multiply ones. $5 \times 1 = 5$.

$$
\begin{array}{r}
301 \\
\times \quad 5 \\
\hline
05
\end{array}
$$

Multiply tens. $5 \times 0 = 0$. Write a zero in the tens place.

$$
\begin{array}{r}
301 \\
\times \quad 5 \\
\hline
1505
\end{array}
$$

Multiply hundreds. $5 \times 3 = 15$.

$$301 \times 5 = 1,505$$

with Zeros

412 × 102

$$\begin{array}{r} 412 \\ \times\ 102 \\ \hline 824 \end{array}$$

Write the problem in columns.
Multiply 412 by the ones digit.
Write the partial product.

The digit in the tens place is a zero. You do not need to write the partial product for tens because it is zero.

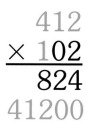

$$\begin{array}{r} 412 \\ \times\ 102 \\ \hline 824 \\ 41200 \end{array}$$

Write a zero in the ones and tens places. Multiply 412 by the hundreds digit. Write the partial product.

$$\begin{array}{r} 412 \\ \times\ 102 \\ \hline 824 \\ +\ 41200 \\ \hline 42024 \end{array}$$

Add the partial products.

$$412 \times 102 = 42{,}024$$

Rounding

You can estimate the answer to a multiplication problem by rounding the larger number.

Estimate 82 × 4.

The greater factor is 82. Estimate 82 × 4 by rounding 82 to the nearest ten, 80.

Drop the zero.	8Ø × 4
Find the basic fact.	8 × 4 = 32
Put the zero back, and add one zero to the answer.	80 × 4 = 320

82 × 4 is about 320.

Does rounding give you a good estimate? Yes. Look at the exact answer.

$$\begin{array}{r} 82 \\ \times\ 4 \\ \hline 8 \end{array} \qquad \begin{array}{r} 82 \\ \times\ 4 \\ \hline 328 \end{array}$$

The estimate, 320, is close to the exact answer, 328.

82 × 4 is exactly 328.

to Estimate

When a problem does not ask for an exact answer, you can use an estimate.

estimate—An answer that is not exact; a reasonable guess.

Adison is running for president of her class. She wants to give each student a flyer. There are 27 students in each of 3 classrooms. About how many flyers should Adison make?

The word *about* tells you that you do not need an exact answer. Estimate the number of flyers Adison needs for three classes.

Round 27 to the nearest ten, 30, then multiply.

Drop the zero. 30×3

Find the basic fact. $3 \times 3 = 9$

Put the zero back, and $30 \times 3 = 90$
add one zero to the answer.

27×3 is about 90.

Adison needs about 90 flyers.

Multiplication

Words that help you know which operation to use to solve math problems are called key words. Some key words for multiplication problems are listed in the table below.

Multiplication Key Words		
at	multiply	rate
each	per	times
every	product	twice

Jennifer is 8. Her brother John is twice as old. How old is John?

The word *twice* tells you that you should multiply by 2 to find John's age.

8 years × 2 = 16 years

Key Words

Some problems will ask you to use the value of one item to find the value of more than one item. For example:

If you know the:	and you need to find the:
Price of one	Price of more than one
Size of one	Size of more than one
Length of one	Length of more than one

you can use multiplication to find the answer.

Keisha wants to buy 6 CDs. Each CD costs $16. How much money does Keisha need to buy 6 CDs?

The word *each* tells you that the price given is for one CD. Keisha wants to buy 6. You know the price of one; you need to find the price of more than one. This is a multiplication problem.

$$\$16 \times 6 = \$96$$

Keisha needs $96 to buy 6 CDs.

Word

The world is full of math problems, but they are usually in the form of word problems. Changing word problems into math is a skill you use every day.

How much juice do you need to fill 24 cups? Each cup holds 8 ounces of juice.

 Read the problem.

What do you know?

There are 24 cups that hold 8 ounces each.

What are you trying to find?

How much juice will you need to fill 24 cups?

 Make a plan.

You are looking for the total amount of juice in 24 cups. You know the amount in one cup and want to know the amount in many cups. This is a multiplication problem.

Problems

3 **Solve the problem.**

Multiply the number of cups by the amount of juice in each.

$$\begin{array}{r} 24 \text{ cups} \\ \times\ 8 \text{ ounces each} \\ \hline 192 \text{ ounces in 24 cups} \end{array}$$

4 **Check your answer.**

Does the answer make sense? *Yes.*
Is the multiplication correct? *Yes.*

Further Reading

Goldish, Meish. *Making Multiplication Easy*.
   New York: Scholastic Press, 1999.

Leedy, Loreen. *2 x 2 = Boo*. New York: Holiday
   House, 1996.

Long, Lynette. *Marvelous Multiplication*.
   Indianapolis: John Wiley & Sons, 2000.

Miller, Marcia, and Martin Lee. *Time Tunes*.
   New York: Scholastic Press, 1999.

Neuschwander, Cindy. *Amanda Bean's Amazing
   Dream: A Mathematical Story*. New York:
   Scholastic Press, 1998.

Internet Addresses

Banfill, J. *AAA Math.* "Multiplication."
© 2000–2002.
<http://www.aaamath.com/mul.html>

The Math Forum. *Ask Dr. Math.* "Elementary
Multiplication." © 1994–2004.
<http://mathforum.org/library/drmath/sets/
elem_multiplication.html>

Index